THE GOOD HOUSEWIFE
Sallets and Salmagundis

DRAWN BY
ROSEMARY SIMMONS

DESCRIBED BY
GILLIAN GOODWIN

'We present you a taste of our English garden housewifery in the matter of sallets.'
JOHN EVELYN: *Acetaria*

THE GELOFER PRESS

To make this condiment your poet begs
The pounded yellow of two hard-boil'd eggs;
Two boiled potatoes, passed through kitchen seive,
Smoothness and softness to the salad give.
Let onion atoms lurk within the bowl,
And, half-suspected, animate the whole.
Of mordant mustard add a single spoon,
Distrust the condiment that bites so soon;
But deem it not, thou man of herbs, a fault
To add a double quantity of salt;
Four times the spoon with oil of Lucca crown,
And twice with vinegar procur'd from town;
And lastly o'er the flavour'd compound toss
A magic soupçon of anchovy sauce.
Oh, green and glorious! Oh, herbaceous treat!
Twould tempt the dying anchorite to eat;
Back to the world he'd turn his fleeting soul,
And plunge his fingers in the salad bowl!
Serenely full, the epicure would say,
'Fate cannot harm me, I have dined today.'
SYDNEY SMITH

Salad

Sallets and salletting, salad as we call it today, has had chequered esteem over the centuries. Vegetables were undoubtedly eaten raw in classical times but they were often blanched and salad included boiled vegetables cooked simply on their own. They were invariably dressed. The counterbalances of dressings on the acid or other qualities of the ingredients were held essential to health. The ancients were very conscious of the influence of diet on health and of the effects of various foods on the body. Mental and physical effects were carefully monitored.

Many people have regarded crudities askance. Lettuce, for example, long recognized as making for somnolence and indeed sometimes called sleepwort, has been distrusted as being bad for poor teeth and, if too much eaten, for the heart. Cresses on the contrary have been thought good for the teeth and for baldness but to make for infertility. Attitudes to cabbage have been mixed. By John Evelyn's time, the seventeenth century, although red cabbage, finely shredded, was eaten raw, our ordinary cabbage was only eaten raw by the Dutch. Cabbage has always been thought windy and Evelyn reckoned it loosening if moderately boiled and astringent if overboiled. But it is difficult to believe that arid Cnidos was famous, along with Praxiteles' Aphrodite, for cooked cabbage; or that crisp Cos lettuce, introduced into England by John Tradescant and used in the Middle East instead of bread for nibbling through a meal, was only served cooked in earlier days.

Palates were subtle in classical times; over-sophisticated some critics maintained. The titillating conglomerations with which some rich citizens flaunted gastronomic rivalry were not dishes of plain living and high thinking. But Plautus' cook protests his discrimination; not for him to serve a pickled meadow for a dinner. Bread, wine and wholesome salads suffice a man, more is luxury, Francis

Bacon quoted Horace approvingly. 'Making an honest meal, and dining upon a sallett, without so much as a grain of exotic spice.' Even with exotic spices some of the dishes of mixed raw and cooked vegetables are refreshing and the Roman cookery book of Apicius which has survived in the guise of later editions gives recipes for moulded salads.

A mixed vegetable dish from the classical tradition. Place a layer of very lightly cooked cabbage chopped after cooking on a layer of well-cooked leek. After dressing this with olive oil, slightly tart wine or very mild vinegar, and cumin (and with *liquamen* for the classical purist but enjoyable without) sprinkle it with very finely chopped raw leek mixed with pepper, caraway and coriander or similar spices. Serve cool. (For *liquamen* see 'Dressings'.)

A sala caccabia. Soak some finely cut slices of good tasty bread without crusts, in a mixture of vinegar and water, squeeze them dry and line an oiled mould. Arrange in the mould layers of a cow's milk cheese, cucumbers, pine nuts and chicken livers sprinkled with chopped capers. Cook covered standing in hot water in a slow oven for half-an-hour. Use the liquidiser to make a sauce (Apicius was famous for his sauces) of pepper, mint, parsley or celery leaves, cheese, pine nuts, dried penny royal (a herb always to be used sparingly for the kidney's sake), honey, vinegar, *liquamen*, hard-boiled egg yolk and water. Pour the sauce over the cooled, turned-out mould, and serve chilled.

From their name these moulded salads would appear to have been cooked but provided ingredients such as chicken livers are cooked first they can be successful with raw ingredients. An advantage of *sala* recipes is that ingredients, quantities and method can be adjusted to suit one's own taste! If fresh mint is not available watercress, for example, can be used. While neither is specially loved by bees, 'apium' is usually translated as celery or parsley. In Roman times celery was smallage, wild celery; the

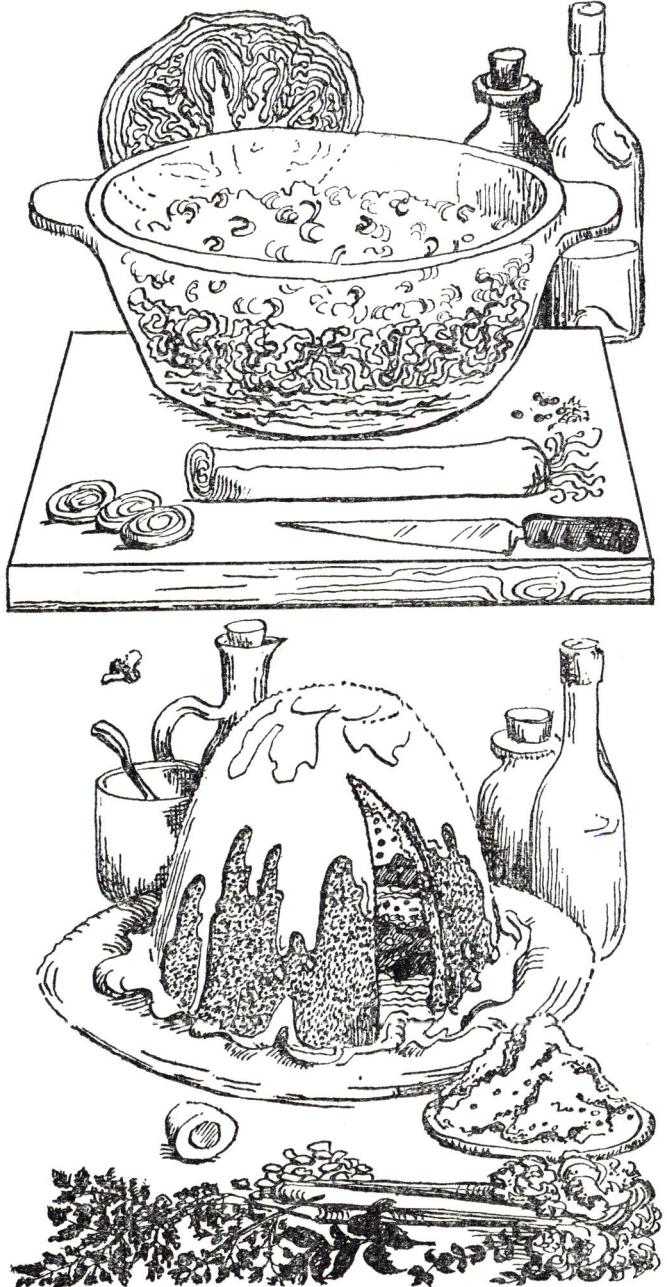

leaves or the seed were used: although cultivated celery is milder its leaves make a reasonable substitute.

An unexpected aspect of Roman cookery is its attractive appearance (Apicius has a general recommendation for keeping vegetables emerald-green by boiling with cooking soda – a mixed legacy to our cuisine) and this *sala* is not only fragrant but pretty.

How far salads can have only raw ingredients and how far they may be cooked has often been debated; some salads, potato or asparagus for example, have always been cooked. In countries where rice provides the staple diet it may be dressed and used in salad. In the Middle Ages and for some time after the arrival of potatoes in Europe, many vegetable dishes which used breadcrumbs for bulk could be regarded as salletting. They still make a useful addition to the cook's repertoire if she makes her own bread; home crumbs are tasty.

The great St Bernard of Clairvaux was a salad man and the Emperor Frederick II was notable for favouring raw salading. Early Italian cookery books list numerous salads. But further north while salads like our 'dips', thick cool sauces, were popular raw vegetables and fruit were distrusted – the use of night-soil was widespread. 'Beware of green salad' wrote John Russell, marshal to Humphrey, Duke of Gloucester, in the fifteenth century, a maxim repeated in Caxton's *Boke of kervynge*. The tradition survived, four hundred years on Surtees has Dr Roger Swizzle helping establish Handley Cross as a spa and recommending a substantial meal by today's standards, 'More people dig their graves with their teeth than we imagine'; he bans salad, cucumbers and celery at dinner.

The *Forme of cury*, King Richard II's roll of recipes and a Cottonian mss. both give only one, similar, salad. However, the saying went that if you did not drink wine after a cold salad you endangered your health and wronged your palate, so salad was eaten. Perhaps it sat uneasily on a stomach filled with widely drunk small ale. In the sixteenth century Dr Andrew Boorde considered that fortified wine could be drunk with salad although not with meat. Fears of salad floating on the digestive tract harked back to antiquity; after wine lettuce swims on the acid stomach, satirised Horace. Over the centuries the health-conscious gourmet has been exercised by this problem of when best to eat salad and the timing has varied from the start through the meal to the finish.

The salad in the 'Forme of cury'. Clean and pluck into small pieces parsley, sage, borage, mint, fennel, cress, rue, rosemary, purslane, chives, garlic, shallot, onion and leek (grown set but most often unset when the blades were cropped daily for the pot). Mix everything together with olive oil, dress with salt and vinegar and serve.

Today we tend to consider salad should be raw or only blanched; from Harrison's *Elizabethan England* we learn it then started a summer supper and from Shakespeare that it had to be young and green. At that time Thomas Tusser's verses list salad herbs with those for sauces. They thus differ from pot herbs which were boiled in the pot along with meat.

'Some are of the opinion that all raw herbs and sallets breed melancholy blood' wrote Robert Burton. And Shirley's wild young man, Fowler, in *The witty fair one* denounces the married state in which he would be '. . . fed upon this or that melancholy dish by prescription, guarded with officious salads, like a prisoner in a throng.' Although this gives a rare indication of how a table was set it is not very complimentary to salad.

In 1629 a year after Shirley's play was licensed John Parkinson published his *Paradisi in sole*. At once an important and a popular book it gave a good deal of attention to salad. It was the usual practice to use wild as well as cultivated plants, taking the young buds and 'putting them all together that the taste of the one may amend the relish of the other.' This is the mixed salad and it could be a very grand affair.

Gervase Markham whose *Way to get wealth* was really how to show you had got it once you had arrived, enabled the aspiring housewife to ape those who actually had a clerk of the kitchen in their household. Having prepared all her salads in advance Markham's housewife was to bring on the grand salad first. This was a mixed salad. It was followed by the boiled salads and finally the smaller mixed salads. Some salads were only for ornament, others were both decorative and to be eaten. Grand compound salads were only for princes or very special occasions.

Even Markham's simple salad was made up of a large number of ingredients while Evelyn's 'all sorts' salad had twenty-four including several flowers and King James II's head gardener is said to have considered there should be at least thirty-five! Possibly he had problems getting sufficient fresh foliage to court each day. Under King George II Bridgeman had to find relays of runners to bring fruit up from the royal gardens to town and few salad or vegetable dishes appear in the guides to table setting. London was growing fast, green stuff was probably only easily obtained in the countryside or country garden whither Evelyn urged his contemporaries and to which, with all his love of gardens, Alexander Pope retreated despondently, leaving Lord Burlington's 'luxurious lobster nights' for 'salads, tarts and pease'.

This had not been the imaginative Parkinson's approach. He suggested planting orange pips and when the seedlings had grown as tall as your finger, plucking them and adding them to a salad to give a fine aromatic and spicy taste; clove gilloflowers, a more fragrant early form of carnation, made a salad in high esteem with the gentry. Unlike some of his contemporaries Parkinson considered spinach fit for salad although, surprisingly, rather tasteless. It was a variety crenellated in leaf like an oak and used for winter salading. Today's spinach salads of North America are far from tasteless. Markham's boiled salad is also a useful way of dealing with spinach for the modern housewife who is not too ardent a feminist.

A simple boiled spinach salad. Chop boiled spinach finely and cook it in butter; stir in currants and vinegar. Season with sugar to suit the taste of the master of the house. Serve with sippets, small pieces of fried or toasted bread.

A compound salad suitable for a great feast. Lay in the bottom of a great dish roughly shredded almonds and figs, stoned raisins, capers, olives and currants, with tender sage and spinach mixed with sugar. Dress this with vinegar and oil and sprinkle it with more sugar, slices of peeled orange and lemon, a layer of finely shredded red cauliflower (a variety of cabbage), a layer of old olives, slices of pickled cucumber and lettuce heart. Serve it prettily using more orange and lemon slices for ornament.

Sweet Cicely: *Myrrhis odorata*
Purslane: *Portulaca oleracea*

Parkinson recommends fresh wakerobin *roots* (the *berries* are *poisonous*) diced into a salad of white endive or lettuce as a way of handling an uninvited guest. This recipe will make a smell-feast over-bold and 'you can have good sport with him.'

John Evelyn is less familiar in his style, as becomes a publicist of culture among the top people. The classic work on salad in English is his delightful monograph *Acetaria*. The dedication is a fine build-up to an excellent recipe for dressing a salad and reflections on exchanging the sceptre for a spade and the purple for a gardener's apron; the country and the salad garden had claimed the major attention of the best magistrates of ancient Rome. In his attempt to establish a status for salad, Evelyn also defined his subject for us.

Sallets consisted of certain succulent plants and herbs, many available from the hedgerow or considered weeds in the garden – here he follows Parkinson, but preferably improved by a gardener – here we have a founder member of the Royal Society. They were to be eaten raw, green or blanched, or candied, whether simply or mixed. They were not to be boiled, baked, pickled or otherwise disguised; these latter were more grateful to the feminine palate!

But even if salad was not suited to her palate salad-gathering was a light summer recreation for a lady. Evelyn took the collecting and mixing of salads as seriously as growing them. He would have no truck with vulgar astrological picking, stipulating that attention be paid instead to the look of the plant.

Nowadays we pick on country walks bright young hawthorn sprouts, bread and cheese, or delicate green leaves of new wood sorrel, then much wild salading was valued. But while every hedge affords a not unagreeable salad ignorance can be fatal and care must be taken not to mistake, for instance, hemlock for salletting; hemlock being not unlike Sweet Cicely, *myrrhis odorata*, the English chervil, in the seventeenth century a most popular salad constituent. Indeed John Gerard in his herbal considers the green seeds far exceed any other salad for taste, smell and wholesomeness.

Evelyn's attention went further; he suggested a particular type of basket for gathering salad which must be plucked delicately and after all the unseemly leaves had been got rid of, cleaned by damping not by sousing, and gently swung in a cloth to dry.

The gifts of the salad maker were displayed in the judicious mixing. A balance of the different humours must be duly attended to, salad vegetables were usually acid and needed skill to mix, while it was important that every plant play its part and neither be overpowered by a particular herb nor strike a jarring note; garlic in salad Evelyn abhorred. But pharmacy was still predominately herbal, he recognized many medicinal qualities in salading and counselled chervil for the aged, noted that rue was said to be good for the sight while mustard was said to be bad.

Although Evelyn leaves an impression of a move to simplicity in salading he could present a grand salad with the best; celery he suggested as an adornment for the centre of a great man's salad, or samphire to which he was partial. Samphire, still found in some parts of the country must have grown more widely for it was once common salading. In spite of the horrors of the task pictured in *King Lear* it seems to have been over-culled: the essayist W. H. Hudson gives us a clue for his old gatherer pulled it up by the root. Shirley's fellow playwright Middleton in *A chaste maid in Cheapside* reckons a wife without a husband is only good for making a salad or crying samphire!

Evelyn's contemporary, Sir William Temple, wrote 'Whoever begins a garden, ought in the first place to consider the soil, upon which the taste of . . . herbs and salads will wholly depend. . . .' Salads would not taste as well grown on clay or rich soil as on sand or gravel although they might be larger and look better. Many gardeners have held that the taste of the fruit could be altered by monkeying with the seed and Googe's translation, *The four books of husbandry*, thought this of lettuce which was also to be prevented from shooting by weighting down, sprinkling with sand to keep it white and tender, as well as, a tiresome chore, tying up two days before gathering to get it rounded.

Not all writers have been so caring of their lettuce. A couple of centuries later the Cambridge professor of botany rudely reckoned that by July lettuce was the offals of the garden only fit for fattening geese; although for August salads he did allow cabbage lettuce, along with celery, endive, nasturtium flowers and blanched sweet fennel. A plot for salad herbs was a recognized part of the kitchen garden and for Evelyn's garden calendar June was the month to sow in it chervil, radish and lettuce, its seedlings were good picked when as broad as a sixpence, just under an inch. He favoured these three for hotbed raising for January eating. They were with purslane the mainstay of salads at the time. Purslane we no longer use. Radishes, to be watered with salt water according to many authorities, now often served on their own were thought comforting to the sated stomach. Chervil is less used today, an omission the good housewife could rectify by growing her own. Lettuce, now our major salading, Leonard Meager thought no garden could be without; he produced it throughout the year at Warkworth.

The dedicated were determined to contrive green salad, the conventional garnish for roast pheasant, in winter. Leonard Meager was a gifted gardener and popular gardening author; his 'secrets known to a very few' successfully obtained salad out of season. It was the period of the foundation of the Royal Society, a technically minded time, and gardeners were much preoccupied with systems of hotbeds for forcing. But before this an early seventeenth-century 'order and government' for a nobleman's house not only proposes 'sallets in store', pickles, for winter fare but also cucumbers and samphire. Hannah Wolley, earliest female precursor of Mrs Beeton, suggests engagingly that for winter salad cabbage shredded finely with a silver knife and then carefully dressed will not be recognized for what it is. Evelyn's 'all sorts' salad was for winter. Most commonly served during winter was lamb's lettuce, corn salad, *valarianella olitoria* or *locusta*; it continued into early spring, a lean time for vegetables. An old Easter dish was red herring, served on corn salad. As unease about potatoes died they were used. Mayonnaise into which mashed potatoes have been beaten makes a good salad. A nineteenth-century recipe most economically soaks the warm potatoes in broth after cooking and before serving, cold, with mayonnaise; it is salutary to realise how often the good housewife of past years cooked vegetables in broth or milk.

Other root vegetables were used in winter salads. In the year Queen Elizabeth I died, Richard Gardiner of Shrewsbury promoting carrots wrote that some would eat them raw and they would digest well in a hungry stomach. Many people, he wrote, wanted red carrots (nowadays yellow are more *récherché*) for their colour, to make dainty salads for roast mutton or lamb, dressed with vinegar and pepper. And Evelyn remarks that the French and Italians carve their beetroot into shapes to ornament a salad: a similar fashion to that of the Sedley household in *Vanity fair* where Mrs Todd who lived in Coram Street and therefore looked up to Russell Square would come in to help out on special occasions for she could make flowers, ducks and so on out of turnips and carrots in a very creditable manner.

Both visual and aromatic aspects were considered by meticulous salad makers who have always had an eye to colour. Violets, marigolds, cowslips and borage are only a few of the bright and scented flowers favoured; after the discovery of north America nasturtiums were popular, their flowers for colour and their seeds for flavour. These flowers were used in mixed salads or as simple salads and in their natural state or preserved in sugar or pickle. Both Robert May in his comprehensive cookery book and Markham have a recipe for presenting a decorative salad of a flower shape made from preserved carnations, cucumber and purslane, 'pretty and curious' for show and use. Pickled ash-keys or broom flowers or the double-blue violets of Mary Doggett's book of receits which are really a sugar preserve gave extra texture as well as colour to a salad.

'They say primroses make a capital salad', said Lord St Jerome in Disraeli's *Lothair*. Lady St Jerome comments 'Barbarian!' But a recipe for Disraeli's primrose salad, said to be his favourite, is given by Mrs Leyel. Known for having triggered off the current enthusiasm for herbs, she also wrote a book only on salad in which she followed Evelyn but included exotics like bananas, guavas and pineapples, far beyond the range of *Acetaria* which hardly gives fruit, apart from melon, a place in salletting. Fruit salads as such appeared on the table only as fresh fruit became less frowned upon and was accepted as a balance to alkalines in diet.

Primrose salad. Gather young shoots of primroses before the leaves develop, tie them in bunches and soak for half-an-hour in salt water; drain; boil for fifteen minutes in lightly salted water. Serve cool with a vinaigrette sauce.

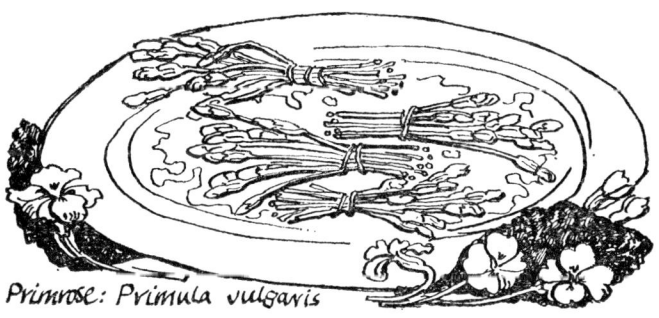
Primrose: Primula vulgaris

Flowers were only one of the devices used by the salad maker to provide a display; there is a 'bird's nest salad' which suggests piquant packaging is an integral part of the American heritage and on occasion salads could be astonishing *tours de force*. John Middleton's newest and best way with a grand salad imitates closely John Nott's spring salad and either is an elaboration anyone might enjoy preparing for the centre of their party table and can be guaranteed sensational.

Bird's nest salad. Rub a little green colouring, artificial or made from spinach, for example, into cream cheese and roll into egg shapes; fleck with pepper to make spots. Arrange lettuce leaves to look like a bird's nest, dress lightly with French dressing, put in the eggs and serve.

A grand spring sallet. Take cowslip and violet buds; the leaves of young lettuce and spinach; Alexander buds; strawberry leaves; water cress; water pimpernel and so on but do not mix them. Then take capers; olives; samphire; cucumber; broom buds; currants and raisins partly boiled to soften them; blanched almonds; barberries and other pickles. Place a turnip or similarly firm vegetable in the middle and form the salad like a castle, making it of pastry (flour and water) brushed over with egg yolk; the pastry to be, surprisingly, of rye flour 'for the honour of the master and benefit of the chef'. Within the castle there should be a tree coloured with green herbs (spinach makes a good green colour) and stuck with flowers in summer or in winter crusted with sugar to look like snow. Twelve pastry supporters are to stand round the castle and four rings of pastry, the biggest on the outside, should mount like steps to the supporters. The different salads should be positioned on the rings and on the rim of the dish a garnish of the pickles.

Middleton who repeats this recipe closely provides the crowning device: the twelve supporters have been reduced to figures representing the four seasons but each of

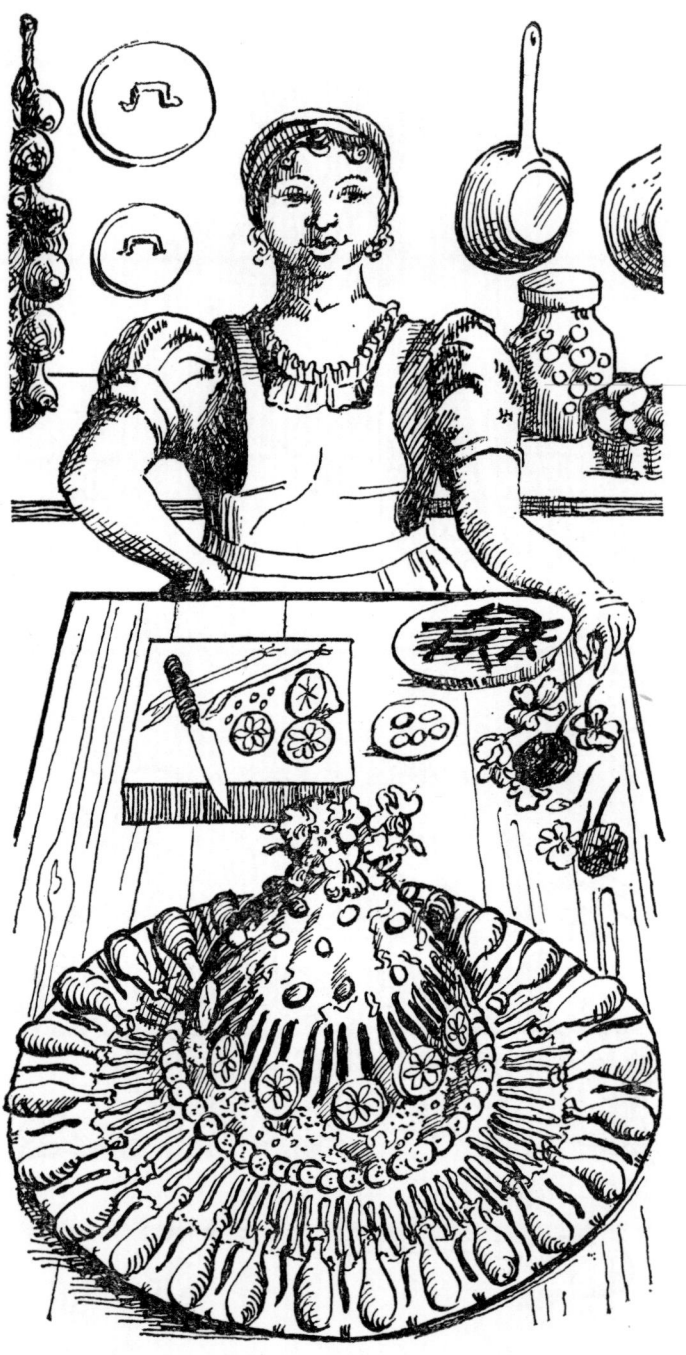

these statues is to hold a cruet in its hand and when everyone is ready to eat the cruets are to be unstoppered and the dressing allowed to run over the salad.

Both Nott and Middleton published cookery books and each was at one time a cook to the Dukes of Bolton; the first duke was notable for travelling round the country feasting at night and clearly kept a sumptuous table. Both cooks give recipes for salmagundis, a sort of salad which would be worth reviving for its name alone but is so suited to our own way of life and so easy to prepare in that the ingredients can be varied as convenient, that its disappearance is astonishing.

Salmagundis

The origin of this splendidly Rabelaisian name is obscure as is the origin of the dish and it has been variously written from salgamaufry to solomon gundy with many versions between. Dr Johnson's definition in about midstream of its popularity is a mixture of chopped meats and pickled herring with oil, vinegar and onions. A mixture of meat and fish is the constant factor and establishes a criterion for the salad. It is a combination of tastes which stretches back to classical cooking and has remained a feature through to *haute cuisine* with its frequent recourse to anchovy essence, denounced by many English cooks. Salmagundis have been aptly described 'mosaics' and when piled up over an inverted pudding bowl are most ornamental.

A salmagundi of John Nott. Beginning at the open end cut a cabbage or Roman lettuce as fine as good big thread and lay a one inch layer in the bottom of a dish. On this lay the breast and wings of two chickens cut in three inch slices, a quarter-inch broad and thin as a shilling, and surround them with slices of boned anchovies. Dice the leg meat and a lemon small and chop four hard-boiled egg yolks with parsley and anchovy and pile all this in the centre of the dish garnishing the pile with little onions boiled very tender and white. Pour over salad dressing, decorate with scalded grapes, French beans or flowers in season and (remarkably) serve hot as a first course.

Another of Nott's salmagundis. Lay in layers in a dish and all finely chopped, roast or boiled chicken or veal; hard-boiled egg yolks and whites, separately; anchovies; lemon pulp; pickles and sorrel, spinach and cloves or finely shredded shallotts. Put a layer of orange or lemon on top; garnish with horseradish, barberries and lemon slices, and dress with a lemon dressing.

There is no suggestion that this or most salmagundis be served hot. Possibly Nott's editing was at fault or the recipe was still becoming established and he had Italian *salmis* in mind. Both Middleton and Nott follow closely on Patrick Lamb but he as befits the master cook to the later Stuart monarchs is less particular in his instructions and more fastidious in his arrangement: he lays his slivers of chicken meat alternately with his anchovies round the edge of the dish like the rays of the sun! So perhaps like so much else on our menus the dish emanated from France and the court of *le roi soleil*.

By 1710 Henry Howard notes great mixed salads going out of fashion: people preferred to mix their own salad on their own plates, dressing them to their own taste. He gives his own salmagundi recipe which, cookery book writers do not change over the centuries, was obviously used by Nott when he addressed the accomplished housewife with meticulous instructions for preparing these versatile creations. The salad with which Alexis Soyer celebrated peace in the Crimea was really a grand salad not a true salmagundi although he did publish a recipe for a game salad which is a very modest version in all but name. Dr Johnson had noted connexions with a sort of Dutch supper of low artisans to which each brought a different dish, an association which may account for this salad's disappearance among the fashionable.

Salad Dressings

Salad was to be dressed delicately, gently stirred until it was all equally moistened. Some people preferred to pour the oil first, alone, as the best way of gilding the leaves with slipperiness. '. . . 'tis incredible how small a quantity of oil', John Evelyn wrote, '. . . is sufficient to imbue a very plentiful assembly of sallet. . . .'

The best oil for salad dressing, Evelyn considered, was pale and green without any scent and as tasteless as possible, such as was made from the olives of Lucca, popular with English tourists at this time. Today, while we may prefer to cook in tasteless oil some people prefer heavier more fragrant oil for salad dressing but it is generally agreed that the first pressing is best.

Other oils are also pressed into use: walnut, more expensively; grapepip, more economically. Some traditional dressings do not use olive oil, which had to be imported, but milk or cream. Thomas Jefferson who was so interested in salad that he grew nineteen varieties of lettuce at Monticello, was also worried by import problems and experimented successfully with sesame oil. With olive oil tantamount to liquid gold some of these recipes are well worth reviving although possibly not a World War II recipe using medicinal paraffin.

Dr Fernie's salad dressing. Mash the yolk of a hard-boiled egg with a teaspoonful each of mustard and brown sugar and half a teaspoonful of salt. Mix in one tablespoonful of vinegar very well before adding three tablespoonfuls of milk.

Olive oil remains supreme as the oil for salad dressing whether in a classic French dressing or a mayonnaise, the sauce traditionally invented by the Duc de Richelieu's chef at the investment of Port Mahon in Minorca, eggs and olive oil being all that was to hand. It became the Edwardian dressing *par excellence* when salad was usually only served with a cold meal. Oil and vinegar appeared

Olive: Olea europaea

on the table so that the diner could dress his salad to his own taste pouring separately from the little bottles or, less genteely, mixing his own dressing in a spoon in an Italian fashion and tossing it with his salad in the crescent-shaped dish curving by the edge of his plate. But liberal helpings with a silver spoon from the boat of mayonnaise was the most frequent choice for dressing the simple mixture of tomatoes and lettuce passed round the table in a glass bowl with, all served separately, very finely sliced, peeled, cucumber, beetroot and celery painstakingly stripped of all stringiness. Thus the riddle, What made the beetroot blush? *It saw the celery strip't*.

While hardly a cold dish from the gourmand books like Mrs Fairclough's *Ideal cookery* would the cook dare send up to the table without its envelopping mayonnaise. When habit cloyed the sauce could be titivated as for example with *puréed* green herbs to become *sauce verte*.

These mayonnaise followed on the popularity of Russian salad, a mixture of diced vegetables, cold meats and shellfish held in a very thick mayonnaise and then set in an aspic-lined mould beautifully decorated. This luxurious and rich contrivance was well suited to the Russian table, that nineteenth-century innovation still disliked by the conservative who resent dining off wood however well-polished and prefer to be served in courses with the dishes on the table rather than from the sideboard.

Egg yolk was included in dressings in John Evelyn's time but it was hard-boiled, although not – they were perfectionists – over-hard or it would not mash into the oil and vinegar satisfactorily. Dressings were runny to trickle over the salading, clinging lightly as they went.

Sugar, Indian salt, was little used in Evelyn's dressings but salt itself was to be clean, bright, dry bay salt, that is salt from the sea-salt pans of the Bay of Biscay.

Pepper always had to be included in a dressing for its heat counter-acted the cold of the salad itself; it was not to be too finely ground or it would stick in the folds of the stomach and be aggravating. Pepper could be ground down from burnet, *pimpinella saxifraga*, but mostly it has always been an import from the east; the most important constituent of all the great spice trade which caused even the Roman empire balance of payment problems.

Mustard was also rarely left out of salad dressing; there were recipes for dried mustard tablets for travellers. The three most esteemed mustards were Tewkesbury, Yorkshire and Dijon. Henry Algernon Percy, Earl of Northumberland, appointing a scullery groom early in the sixteenth century, took care to choose a man who could mix his mustard well. Not only was vinegar kept in the scullery, so was the silver, and the scullery groom had to check it after every meal: his was a responsible job and the fifth Earl evidently took his mustard seriously. There was plenty of instruction available if you wished to make your own and Sir Hugh Platt strongly recommended doing so because the vinegar used in bought made-up mustard would turn your stomach if you saw it. By Sydney Smith's day vinegar was evidently obtained from London even by gourmets.

Lady Holmeby's mustard. Dry true mustard seed in a cooling bread oven. Beat and sift it to the finest powder and mix it very well with sherry to a consistency which suits you adding a little fine sugar to taste and, if you like, a very little wine vinegar.

John Evelyn's mustard. Use Tewkesbury or the best Yorkshire seed exquisitely sifted, winnowed, freed from husks by cutting it in water and not over-dried. Mix this to a pulp with vinegar in which you have steeped grated horse-radish.

Vinegar, the other essential ingredient which gives a dressing sharpness, unless lemon is used, provides more scope for the good housewife who once she has dabbled with making her own will be reluctant to return to commercial brands. Sir Hugh Platt's comments on purchased mustard, as well as economy, sufficiently account for the numerous recipes in early housewifery manuals. You can even make instant dried vinegar for travelling.

Many of the recipes use raisins as a base. Spring water and raisins were corked in stone bottles and left in the warm from May to Michaelmas. The liquor, still thick and heavy, was then transferred to an iron-hooped tun and left to settle for three months. After this it could be drawn off. It was generally considered that the best vinegar came from the middle of the barrel, thus the bung was at lower middle level. The remarkable Sir Dudley North, brother to Charles II's Lord Chancellor, made his own vinegar with typical intelligence and enthusiasm. He used three containers: in the first which was always foul and thick and always replenished was the fruit; the liquor was refined in the second vessel and was finally drawn off into the third from which it was taken as required.

Travellers' vinegar. Mix a paste of green wheat or rye and very strong vinegar. Roll it into balls and dry them in the sun. When needed dissolve a bit in wine.

Experienced and habitual vinegar makers treasure their own 'mother', the thick cloudy jelly which forms on the alcohol being used to make the vinegar and which, like a yoghurt culture, enables them to establish their own speciality. Delicate and tasty vinegars can be made easily in the modern home which is usually warm. Expansive vinegar making involving a wide surface for aeration may not be so easy but the end of a decanter of wine, lees or better still the dregs of a cask of real country cider bottled with non-metallic screw tops and kept warm for six months make excellent vinegars which will revolutionise salad dressing. Samphire was often used to flavour vinegar and sprigs of rosemary, tarragon or so on can be stuck palatably into the bottles in spite of the poet Boileau,

> *A costé de ce plat paroissoient deux salades,*
> *L'une de pourpier jaune et l'autre d'herbes fades,*
> *Dont l'huile de fort loin saissoit l'odorat,*
> *Et nageoit dans des flots de vinaigre rosat.*

As the Armada sailed, rose vinegar would have been in every good housewife's closet; made from damask roses it was thought to be less constipating than from red, from white it was loosening. This was in the tradition of earlier doctoring. The influential and in its day advanced medical school of Salerno whose precepts were put into English by a godson of Queen Elizabeth I considered vinegar lessened fertility but increased appetite. A horrifying medicine, a sort of vinegar cure, was taken by Dorothy Osborne. Overnight she left a piece of steel in white wine which she drank next morning and not surprisingly felt sick for two hours.

The dangers of vinegar and metal in contact were recognized if not understood. Evelyn is firm that salad must be dressed in a porcelain bowl, although glass was an acceptable alternative. Our modern wood appears not to have been considered, presumably wooden ware was for the poor.

Instead of flower-flavoured vinegars flower waters were sometimes used to dress salad. As the exhaustive repast in

Peter Erondelle's instructive *The French garden* begins, the butler is charged with making sure the silver bottle of rosewater has been set on the table. If banqueting dishes were sprinkled with rosewater infused with oil of nutmeg the scent would be as pleasing as the taste, said the cooks.

A rosewater. Collect two pounds of scented rose petals before they fall and put them into earthenware or a stainless steel saucepan and cover with cold soft water. Bring slowly to the boil, leave until cold and strain.

But for dressing salad wine vinegar has usually been preferred to all others including malt, that traditional English vinegar of pub pickles and chip potatoes. How many of us as we follow our forebears and sprinkle vinegar on our fish and chips are aware that the Roman cookery book recommends preserving fried fish by pouring hot vinegar on them the moment they come out of the frying pan?

Vinegar was not only mixed with oil in salad dressing. Evelyn's 'all sorts salad' was served with flowers and vinegar in little china saucers. When the Erondelle meal moves on to the fish course fresh vinegar is put into the diners' saucers reminding us that the biblical Ruth, like Erondelle an alien, was graciously told by Boaz she might eat bread and dip her morsel into the vinegar with his people. For centuries vinegar was a widely used disinfectant. The Roman army's water ration was laced with mild vinegar; it was considered refreshing and the jeering soldier of the crucifixion is currently thought to have been kindly in offering Jesus a spongeful of his *posca*.

But the dressing most widely used in Roman times was *liquamen* sprinkled ubiquitously and giving rise to derogatory comments on the taste of the time. Yet the sophisticated cuisine of the Baghdad of the *Arabian nights* used liberal sprinklings of rose water and the most fastidious culinary critic today is likely to have a high regard for Chinese cooking where soya plays a similar role. Recipes for making *liquamen* have survived. It was economical for it used the entrails of larger fish or the small fish that got caught up in the fishermen's nets, salted and sun-dried. It was mass-produced in factories but can easily be made at home although it is smelly. The basic sauce was varied by extra reducing or additions, often *defrutum*, must boiled down by a third. Recent editors of Apicius have used grapejuice instead of must.

Liquamen. Use small pieces of dried fish in plain water (this will become very salty on reduction) or fresh fish scraps in a strong brine (strong enough to sustain a small egg); add origanum (marjoram), boil and reduce by about a third. When cooled strain through muslin and store well-sealed for it is very pungent. If it is too strong in use it can be let down with a little water, and honey will take the edge off the saltiness.

Roman salad dressings. For cucumber. Peppercorns and penny-royal ground in a mortar and added to a mixture of honey, *liquamen* and wine vinegar. *For endive.* Oil, wine and finely chopped onion. In winter when endive was used instead of lettuce it was dressed with honey and vinegar.

In the Middle Ages cooked salads were often dressed with verjuice made from crab apples, unripe pears or grapes. Where these are not available a pleasant substitute is the juice of cooking apples and lemons mixed. Saffron, considered particularly good for health, was popular with the Germans who made little dried saffron balls which they crumbled on their salads; later, Evelyn disapproved of this as over-powering.

Nearer our own day, the Reverend gourmet Sydney Smith's salad dressing was more judicious and if he came across potatoes used like this it is no wonder William Cobbett bridled that he did not regard them as inedible filth, they made an acceptable sauce but were no substitute for bread. But then Sydney Smith prided himself on his salad mixing, and his dressing becomes someone whose idea of heaven was to eat *paté de foie gras* to the sound of trumpets.

'Very excellent' salad dressing. Sydney Smith to Lady Holland: Oil 4 Tables; Vinegar 2; Salt 3 Tea spoons; Essence of Anchovy 1; Mustard 1; the Yellow of two Eggs boild hard; 2 or 3 potatoes boild and straind through a Sieve; ½ a Tea Spoon of onion chopped very fine. Mix the salad thoroughly just before it is used.

Also published by The Gelofer Press
THE GOOD HOUSEWIFE
SCENTS AND AROMATICS
Drawn by Rosemary Simmons
and described by Gillian Goodwin

© Rosemary Simmons and Gillian Goodwin 1980
ISBN 0 9506529 1 1
The Gelofer Press, 29 Chalcot Square, London NW1
Printed in England by The Stellar Press Limited